Minimalism

Learn How To Transcend The Practices Of Organizing And Minimalism In Order To Eradicate Household Tasks, Allowing You To Reduce The Amount Of Cleaning Required And Enjoy A More Fulfilling Lifestyle

HOWARD BALDWIN

TABLE OF CONTENT

What Is Minimalism? 1

The Whole Advantages Of Living A Minimalist Lifestyle 13

Prioritise Saving And Spend Later. 20

How A Minimalistic Life Can Improve Yours .. 23

How To Make Your House Less Cluttered 33

The Reasons For Reading This Book 51

Learning About The Minimalist Theory 57

Other Types Of Decluttering 72

The Goods And Bads Of Minimalism 77

Release Time From Your Schedule 90

Give Your Life Purpose And Unique Meaning 108

What Is Minimalism?

Simply put, minimalism is the practice of minimising your purchases, debt, and stress to make the most of what you already have. Setting priorities is the key. It's essential to understand what you own and why. When you opened a package, have you ever discovered anything you forgot you had?

That's a positive indication that embracing a minimalist lifestyle will benefit you.

This does not imply that you should begin discarding items without further thought. That's the antithesis of minimalism. It is inefficient and may make you feel like you are punishing yourself. If you just start tossing things away, your friends and family will get your mind examined as the first thing they do.

Obtaining more time, money, and space is the aim. By releasing all that is pulling you down, you will be able to do this.

Consider this. Envision yourself within a vacant walk-in wardrobe. When you first enter, the space appears enormous. You begin mentally sketching it out out of instinct. You consider the beauty of it and decide you want your shoes and shelves here. Next, you start constructing the frames.

Although the area appears more constrained, you may joyfully envision how you want it to be. You think the wardrobe looks impressive after taking a closer look. You then begin to pack your belongings into it. First, your shoes.Next, your attire. It seems highly cosy right now. Before you know it, you're scanning the area and wondering if your partner would mind storing their belongings in the smaller closet down the hallway.

Now, the enormous area isn't quite large enough. Has the room's dimensions changed? Was additional space created by having different storage options? What genuinely altered? It was your way of thinking. It was the way you thought about that closet.

That's how life is. We believe that is everything we can do. We experience tension and exhaustion. That closet is us. We feel liberated and limitless as long as we don't overcrowd our lives with so much stuff that it's closing in on us. We start to restrict and create boundaries for ourselves when we overburden ourselves with possessions.

What is the minimalist movement?

It's about clearing your body, mind, and soul of the debris of daily life to make room for the things that truly matter to you. It is about taking charge of your destiny. It is self-forgiveness. It involves removing stuff you no longer need, even sentimental items that may bring back memories.

If you are clinging to the past and the memories it contains, how can you move on to a future full of experiences?

How much does a simple lifestyle require?

Self-liberation requires commitment. To identify what prevents you from reaching your full potential, you must examine your life honestly. Sometimes, you have to be brutally honest. It implies you need to give up giving reasons. It means you must look in the mirror and adjust what you find objectionable.

Although it's not always a straightforward procedure, and you might want to give up, there are a lot of benefits. Less worry, financial independence, and more family time are the benefits. Nothing else in life can provide this level of contentment. Even those who are financially independent lament their excessive stress levels. Money cannot purchase happiness.

Who is capable of leading a simple life?

Everyone can lead a basic lifestyle. You can attain minimalism if you take a serious, in-depth look at your life and everything in it. You can get minimalism if you know what to do.

Thus, simply take some time to determine that you are prepared to make significant changes, and then begin with the first action.

Making a decision is the first thing you need to do. Next, you must enlist the support of your family. Before moving things out of the house, involve your family. No matter how much you purge, it makes no difference if your family keeps adding new items to the home.

This may entail asking grandparents to refrain from purchasing unnecessary apparel or an excessive number of toys. It can cause you to exert more pressure than you are accustomed to.

For Elderly Kids

Taking an older child shopping can be rather challenging when they want everything. Even with a big budget, it might get old quickly. Refusing to give anything to them is the most straightforward approach to show kids that they cannot have everything. This is one of those things that is easier said than done.

But from the moment you create your list, inform them that you will only buy what is on it and follow through. Allowing children to assist you in making the list is one way to involve them. As you compile your list, educate them on the distinction between needs and wants.

Ask them to check the refrigerator, for instance, and tell them what you are missing. While cookies are a wish, milk is a must. Just buy the items on the list when you visit the store. Don't get anything if it's not on the list, even if you need it. Ask them if it's on the list when they make a request. Inform them no if they respond negatively. They will eventually realise we don't need it, so we won't purchase it.

Go out of the store, as for those meltdowns. Go to your car after leaving your full basket where it is. They go home after continuing to act out.

Once they settle down, go back to shopping. When you go home, and they're not eating what they requested, tell them you were unable to complete your shopping because they wouldn't cooperate.

They'll quickly realise that going shopping is essential. It requires endurance and patience. They will eventually come to comprehend.

For Young Adults and Teens

It might be hard for a child to know what they truly need and want when they have grown up with everything they could wish to bought for them. Consider offering them a stipend. Inform them that you will care for the necessities and that they may get anything else independently.

They will come to understand what they truly need and desire. They will learn not to waste anything from it. Additionally, it will get them ready to take on independent duties.

Teens who work should be given some responsibility as soon as they start working. They ought to be able to cover the cost of petrol if they are driving. They ought to assist with insurance. If they're working, that is.

I know of one mom who had to teach her child the hard way how costly petrol may get. She was frequently asked to take her pals around because she was the only one among them who could drive. She was begging for more money for petrol all the time.

Her parents initially believed that she had to do it to get to school. It was just too pricey after a time. So, her folks would take her car every Sunday night and fill it up. That was it till Sunday the following week when the petrol ran out. It would have to be the bus for her. The daughter would run out of petrol, so she first used the bus two or three days a week.

She ran out of petrol multiple times, forcing her to spend the weekends at home. She eventually figured out how to get her buddies to pitch in for gas. She stopped using the bus in a short amount of time. Sometimes, it's necessary to learn a lesson the hard way.

Determine how to inspire them.

Decluttering your home can begin once your family has decided on the scope and schedule of the minimising process. Even though your kids initially consented to the idea during the family meeting, the initial decluttering will probably take several days and numerous decluttering sessions, which will certainly leave them with a bad taste in their mouths.

So, figure out how to entertain the whole family. Provide a prize for taking part, such as treating them to a special meal after a hard day of organising. Once the entire house has been decluttered, you may even treat your family to a vacation. Play lively, enjoyable music throughout your decluttering sessions to lighten everyone's attitude and make the process enjoyable rather than tedious.

Focusing on what your children want to keep rather than what they want to get rid of is another tactic you might want to try, particularly when helping them get rid of their toys. Ask them to sort items into piles that they wish to keep, and then dispose of the others without fuss. Focus as much as you can on the benefits of minimization and try not to dwell on the items you're losing.

Instruct them to consider others.

Encourage your children to sort through their belongings and think about what they could be able to donate to a child in need of toys. Inform them that there are young people without toys in their own towns and neighbourhoods. When you're ready to part with the toys permanently, find a place to donate them so that children in need can receive them, and bring your kids along when you make the donation. Your children will be much more motivated and will learn to help others if they can see where their toys are going and understand that even a modest sacrifice will make a big difference in someone else's life.

Give them the option.

Allow your children to pick as much as they can as long as it stays within the rules you've established (more on that in the following chapter). Not only will you win your kids over by letting them choose what they want to keep, but it will also instill in them a feeling of responsibility and ownership over their possessions.

It might be challenging to convince your family to minimise, particularly if you have children. Although it can be difficult to persuade someone to part with treasured belongings, the process will go much more smoothly if you're ready to address their concerns, make concessions when needed, and come up with entertaining ways to keep them motivated. Establishing rules for the items your family choose to keep and how they will be handled should be a part of your preparedness; we'll cover all of this in the upcoming chapter.

The Whole Advantages Of Living A Minimalist Lifestyle

Please complete this exercise in this chapter. Consider a home where each room is covered in patterned wallpaper. Suppose all the rooms have patterned carpets and the colours don't go well together. The colour of the sofa is dark. When you enter the room, the colour of the walls and the black drapes immediately catch your attention. There are numerous ornaments scattered about, and dust gathers on them all. A few of them date back to the days when the children went on field trips. Some are presents from folks who felt they had good taste. For a brief period, close your eyes and visualise this kind of setting. When faced with a room like this, let alone a mansion full of them, you get the impression that the mind can never find a place to relax. Every room is so crowded that it is difficult to unwind. It is so full of stuff that it is difficult to settle down since you are constantly feeling bad about the condition of the house and the possessions inside.

This may be an exaggeration, but I use it to illustrate the idea that "less is more" as I describe what it's like, on the other hand, to enter a neatly organised home that isn't overly furnished or cluttered. A hotel room is often colourless. It usually has few personal touches and is friendly. You quickly realise that you are away from home, but if you pay a reasonable fee for a hotel room, it will be simple, clean, and most definitely functional. This is a step below your home. In addition to being tidy and functional, it should be cosy and include some of your most treasured possessions. One item that can assist you in the declutteringprocess is referred to as a focal point. Close the door and leave the room where you are going to clear. Next, walk inside the room and genuinely observe what draws your attention right away. It ought to be the main attraction. For a minimalist family, it may be an artwork. It could be a brightly coloured vase or a plant. But when you walk into a room in your house, the abundance of clutter draws your eyes in all directions and makes it difficult to find the area's focal point.

When you declutter, you refocus everything and intentionally set up your space to function as you did when you originally moved into the house. You purge unnecessary things and confirm that everything in the space is meant to be there. You will find your focus points right away and find the space enjoyable, but first, you must win over the entire family. You must establish the following guidelines at home if you want to maintain your minimalist lifestyle:

A room is usually left in a more orderly state after people depart it.

After taking a bath, folks tidy up and put their laundry in the trash.

When using the loo, individuals use the brush to ensure that it is clean for the person using it after them.

A child has to give up one old toy in order to receive a new one.

Teens have to determine what to give up before they can receive anything new.

If children understand that doing this will enable them to follow your example and keep their rooms clean, they are unlikely to rebel against you despite your fears. To make it easier for young children to maintain a clean and organised bedroom, consider giving them access to easy-to-access storage. Teens who are allowed this independence have been shown to maintain their rooms cleaner than those who do not, therefore supporting the concept of allowing them to choose the colour scheme for their room and encouraging them to have their own style.

Children who learn to cook will inherit valuable skills and understand the importance of consuming high-quality food rather than constantly turning to unhealthy, convenient options. They also enjoy participating in garage sales to raise money for new toys, and they will quickly learn the lesson of excess if it is established that each item that is brought in must be replaced by one or two that are taken out.

Your home will have a better atmosphere, and you won't feel as pressured every day after work. Because you won't have as much housework to do, you'll have more time to spend with your children and truly enjoy your vacation. Make use of part of this time to take the kids on a field trip or to a country setting so they can enjoy the outdoors and get enough exercise. Living a simple lifestyle will prevent kids from losing themselves in front of a computer screen and increase their interest in the world around them.

The benefits of minimalism are numerous. It facilitates easier living. It gives your house a brand-new, modern feel. It relieves a lot of your tension related to chores and responsibilities and turns your house into a delightful place where you can invite guests over on a whim without worrying about cleaning up after them. Additionally, you'll notice that your chances of entertaining and hosting people at your freshly decorated house have increased significantly. If you demonstrate the advantages to them, they're likely to change their way of living as well because a minimalist home is amazing.

Prioritise Saving And Spend Later.

Spending more than you make is just part of the modern culture. Every belief—whether to purchase a fancy automobile, have a large mortgage, or splurge on expensive meals and travel—indicates that you should spend more money than you make.

When someone is engaged in the saving is the last thing on their mind. With the leverage that the person exercises, the treadmill starts itself, and the spiralling credit card debt that results from the high-interest rates that banks charge on it picks up speed.

Nobody can argue against someone choosing to live a particular lifestyle; it's their choice. Learning things on your own is a fundamental component of free will. This book confines our discussion to the goal of financial freedom. If one is interested in financial independence, the ultimate poison is an excessive spending habit.

To achieve financial independence, the person is primarily concerned with accumulating a sizeable sum of money that would eventually enable him to generate a cash flow from the returns on his investments and eliminate the need for a fixed salary.

A person who aspires to financial independence saves first and spends the remaining earnings, as Warren Buffett stated in the quotation above. This gives the impression of scarcity and discipline, enabling the person to survive on a limited budget. If someone trains themselves to live on 0.8X over time while earning X, it is conceivable to accomplish so. The remaining 20% of monthly savings, which will add up over time, goes towards the fund for financial freedom.

What qualities distinguish those who use this tactic, and how do they ensure its success? Here are a few observations.

How A Minimalistic Life Can Improve Yours

Living A Simpler Existence Free From The Shackles Of Possessions And Minimalism Has Many Benefits Beyond Just Relieving Stress. Though That Is A Huge Plus, Decluttering Your Home Is About More Than Just Not Stabbing Your Toe When You Try To Urinate At Three In The Morning.

Less Goods Equates To Less Debt, And Debt Reduction Leads To Increased Financial Independence. After You Pay Off The Credit Card In Full, Stop Using It. We're Not Advocating For You To Give Up On Your Education Loans And Sell Everything You Own; Rather, We're Talking About Considering If You Really Need That New, Pricey Jacket You Were Ready To Charge To Your Credit Card. Even Though Your Monthly Credit Card Payment May Only Be $15, Interest And Credit Card Fees Can Quickly Add Up, Turning That $100 Jacket Into A $150

One—All At The Cost Of Not Having To Pay The Full Amount Upfront.

Would You Have Paid The Money In Full If That Was Your Only Option? If Yes, What Is The Initial Reason For Using The Credit Card? If Not, You Have Spared Not Just The $100 That You Would Have Otherwise Paid In Interest And Fees But Also The Additional $50 That You Would Have Lost.

Less Stuff Means More Money To Spend On The Adventures You've Always Wanted To Take Part In, Like Kayaking In Yellowstone Or Traveling To Ireland.

You Might Even Use That Money To Start Saving For Your Own House. Nobody Is Suggesting To You That Buying A House Is A Needless Financial Expenditure.

Adopting A Minimalist Mindset And Way Of Living Can Also Benefit The Environment. You Will Have Less To Replace Or Discard If You Own Fewer Items. Reducing The Amount Of Possessions And "Necessary Stuff" We Use Can Help Lessen Our Environmental

Impact And Maintain The Health Of The World Where We Live. Constant Consumerism Is Thought To Be Destroying The Environment Around Us. Reduced Product Consumption Results In Less Pollution Entering The Environment And Fewer Resources Needing To Be Used To Produce The Mounting Things.

Time To Be More Productive Also Comes With This Minimalist Way Of Living. Less Distracting And Time-Consuming Items Around You Will Allow You To Focus More Of Your Time And Attention On Things That Are Actually Important. Eliminating Consumerist Distractions From Your Life Can Improve Your Quality Of Life Because It Replaces One Source Of Attention With Another, Whether That Be Spending Time With Friends And Family, Going For A Walk In Your Favorite Spot, Or Working On That Necessary Task In A Place That Makes You Smile. You Can Incorporate So Many Activities That Improve Your Current Life Into That Extra Time; For Example, Yoga,

Meditation, Exercise, Gardening, Hiking, And Even Fishing And Hunting Are All Considered Stress-Relieving Hobbies That Many People Just "Do Not Have Time For."

By Giving Away And Eliminating Items You Eventually Do Not Need, You Can Clear Your Mind Of Any Distractions And Free Up Time For These Kinds Of Activities That Can Help You Feel Less Stressed.

Furthermore, You May Be Confident That You Are Leading By Example For A Large Number Of People. If You Are A Parent, Your Kids Will Observe Your Behavior And Take After You, Modeling Your Way Of Living. If You Detest The Way You Spend Money When You Shop, But Your Children Witness You Doing It, They Will Develop The Same Spending Habits As You And Experience Similar Problems In Later Life.

However, If You Can Overcome Those Obstacles And Live A Less Stressful Life, You'll Impart To Your Kids The Idea That This Is How Life Should Be Lived.

Friends, Coworkers, And Even Other Family Members Like Your Parents May Be Impacted By The Same Effect. In This Section Of The Book, The Adage "Be The Change You Wish To See In The World" Is Extremely Accurate, As Modeling Change For Those Around You Is The Most Effective Approach To Affect Change In Others. Do It Yourself Rather Than Discussing It, Considering Whether To Do It And Then Telling Others It's A Wonderful Idea. Allow The Transformation In Your Life To Serve As The Tangible Evidence That Others Require To Make The Same Shift In Their Own Lives.

The Fact That Leading A Simple Lifestyle Replenishes Your Energy Reserves Is Another Wonderful Benefit. Seeing The Mess All Around Them As They Enter Their Houses Acts As A Reminder To Many That There Are Things They Are Letting Go Of. The Mess May Act As A Constant Reminder That We Need To Prioritize Other Areas Of Our Lives Above Others Or That We Are Perpetually Behind On Something.

Furthermore, Belongings Have A Strange Ability To Ingrain Us In Places We Don't Need To Be. Because We Do Not Want To Deal With The Mess Of Clutter That Exists Within Our Houses, Having Too Much Stuff Can Almost Make It Feel Like A Nuisance To Apply For That New Job And Relocate To Another State To Take It.

We Then Use Our Belongings And Clutter As The Excuse For Not Being Able To Accept The Job That Would Clearly Make Us Happier At This Time, Even Though The Income Is A Little Less.

Your Belongings Are "Rooting You Down," So How Much Life Are You Actually Missing Out On?

When You Have Less Of Them, You Are More Inclined To Move, Travel, And Discover Places That Might Eventually Lead To Your Happiness And To Take Those Risks.

However, Escaping The "Comparison Game" Is One Of The Biggest Advantages Of Leading A Minimalist Lifestyle. In Modern Society, The Possessions We Own Serve As Markers Of Our Social

Standing, Prosperity, And Self-Worth. Children Are Graded In Middle School Based On What They Wear And Whether Or Not It Is A Name Brand. Teens Are Graded In High School According To The Gadgets They Own, Including Whether Or Not They Have The Newest Iphone Model. The Rating And Comparing Game Persists In The Adult World.

Step 2: Make Your House Simpler

You Might Need Some Time To Adjust To Living In A Minimalist House, But In The End, You'll Be Happy You Made The Move. However, Keeping Up With Household Maintenance And Creating The Proper Habits To Minimize Duties Requires Discipline And Work.

It Would Be Helpful To Have An Idea Of The Typical Design Of A Minimalist Home In Order To Create A Minimalist System For Housekeeping. The Following Are Some Attributes You Should Strive For:

Pieces Of Furniture That Are Necessities. The Only Objects In Any Area Are Those That Are Truly Utilized, Not Just Decorative Pieces. A Minimalist

Kitchen, For Instance, Might Contain A Sink, Stove, Refrigerator, And A Shelf To Accommodate The Same Amount Of Crockery As The Occupants.

Clean Surfaces. Except For A Few Necessary Items Like A Light Or A Container Of Flowers, If It Makes You Happy, Flat Surfaces Like Floors And Tables Are Usually Clear. Nor Even A Pile Of Books Or Papers, Nor Even Other Random Curios.

Gentle, Harmonious Hues. The Fundamentals Will Shine Out In A Room When Simple Colors Are Used. White, For Example, Has Long Been A Classic Minimalist Mainstay Because It Elongates Small Spaces And Is Such A Calming Color That You Can Relax And Decompress Just By Gazing At It. Of Course, In Addition To White, You May Also Go With Other Muted Hues Like Green, Beige, And Blue.

Thoughtful Accents. While The Main Goal Of Minimalism Is To Maintain The Necessities, You May Still Appreciate The Artwork And Vibrant Colors. You May, For Example, Leave Much Of Your

Wall Empty Save For A Framed Family Portrait Or An Original Painting. Additionally, You Can Add Accent Pieces To Your Home To Create A Cozier Atmosphere, Such As A Crimson Pillow To Go With Your Plain White Couch Or A Potted Plant.

Every Object Has A Location. Maintenance Will Be Simple If You Assign A Specific Location For Everything You Own. Since You Will Have Fewer Things, Keeping Them All Organized Will Not Be Difficult. Ensure That The Products Are Arranged In The Locations That Work Best For You. For Instance, Make Sure To Keep Items You Use Frequently Handy And Store Items You Use Infrequently On A Shelf Or In A Drawer.

It's Not Necessary For Your Property To Become A Minimalist Residence Overnight. On The Other Hand, You Can Use Your Intense Passion For This Change As Motivation To Simplify, Clean, Rearrange, And Declutter. Ultimately, What Matters Most Is That You Feel

Comfortable, Secure, And Happy In Your Own House.

How To Make Your House Less Cluttered

Decluttering their home is often the first step towards leading a more minimalist lifestyle. Some people only take this one step, but we urge you to adopt a decluttering mindset all your life long. Many people are unaware of the tension that comes with possessing too many possessions. Disorganized and superfluous objects in our lives can lead to pressures that give us the impression that we ultimately do not have control, whether you are the type of person who continuously stubbles your pinky toe against the leg of that chair or who gets stressed out by all the books and papers in your office.

However, you are in charge.

Although it may seem easy enough, clearing up clutter in your home may rapidly become a difficult task for everyone who tries it. Whether an inanimate object represents a positive or negative aspect of our past, humans have a tendency to attach emotional sentiment to it. This tendency alone can keep us from taking the necessary actions to free ourselves from the clutter that exists in our closets, let alone the clutter that takes up entire rooms.

Making sure you know the difference between preserving memories and preserving emotions should be your first step. Positive memories are stored in photo albums, picture frames, and little mementos. These are objects that bring back memories of times and people in our past. Eliminating these photos and priceless memories does not constitute decluttering a house. But your child's first crib and their homecoming costume are not the same thing.

The first is the size itself. The distinction between emotional and memory attachment is the other, though.

Looking at an object, such as a picture or the first garment your child wore home, can evoke memories of a specific physical place, person, and moment in time. This phenomenon is known as memory attachment. When you gaze at an item, such as a couch, cot, or antiquated piece of memorabilia, and you are reminded of the feeling that once surrounded it, that is known as an emotional attachment. You can still clearly recall the first time you placed your child in their cot. You recall those tearful mornings when you had to wake up at all hours of the night to tend to your ailing child. You recall when they eventually outgrew their cot.

One is associated with a specific moment, whereas the other is associated with numerous moments that elicit strong emotional reactions.

Since it will initially be difficult to tell the two apart, some people arrange objects just by size. But this is really the distinction you are making: an object you keep tends to be associated with a single event, while an item you give away tends to evoke memories of several other occasions.

Do not panic; it will arrive in due course.

Getting assistance from someone is the best advice you can give to tidy your home. When it comes to holding that leather jacket you bought two years ago for an excursion you never went on; they will offer an unbiased evaluation. The tag is still on it. They will help you stay focused on your final objective while recognizing when giving anything away can be excessive.

Another thing to know is that, for many individuals, decluttering a home happens in phases rather than all at once.

It's difficult to let go of these emotional ties, which is one of the numerous reasons that our "things" cause us so much stress. Surrounding ourselves with objects that consistently elicit a range of emotions is taxing on our limbic systems, adrenal glands, and neural connections. For most people, feeling emotionally exhausted is just part of who they are, and they are often unaware of it!

Thus, begin in a single room. Make it your mission to declutter any space in your house by the end of the day. To raise money for other, more important things (like those pesky bills we all have to pay), bring in boxes and donate materials, or even organize a huge yard sale.

Next, proceed room by room and discard anything superfluous that you can live without for the time being. If anything is too deeply ingrained in your prior experiences for you to let go of just yet, try not to freak out and put yourself through unnecessary stress. Many discover that it will take two or three iterations to fully get rid of everything cluttering their houses, even when decluttering room by room.

Decluttering can involve organizing items as well as getting rid of them. In order to have records available for everything crucial they interact with, including their cars, health care, medical bills, and critical documents, many people still use paperwork. Even while leading a minimalist lifestyle might be quite affordable, there are instances when you need to make a purchase to keep organized. Investing in a filing cabinet or hanging file folders that fit into empty pull-out cabinets is a reasonably priced way to gather all of those crucial documents that are strewn all over the place and keep them somewhere you can readily access.

Decluttering closets may prove to be the most difficult task for some individuals. Some people's wardrobes are naturally large, while others are naturally small. In the event that your closet is naturally spacious, consider the following advice for organizing your clothes: Take out a bin, place it behind you, and start carefully removing each article of clothes one at a time. Throw it in the trash and throw it behind your head if you haven't worn it in a year. You can sell or donate these items of clothing, and it will assist you in determining what you actually wear and what you just hang onto because you can.

Using number-based methods is another approach to simplify your house. You can go through your house as long as you need to, load up a garbage bag with items you no longer need, and then donate or discard them. Another option is to participate in the 12-12-12 Challenge, which involves going through your house and identifying 12 items that you can give, 12 items that you can discard, and 12 items that can be put back in their rightful places. Many people find that playing these number games helps them keep their emotional attachments to several random objects in check by shifting the focus from the item to the counting correlation.

Creating a list is yet another piece of advice that you can use. For other people, the thought of starting to clear each space is too much to handle. Perhaps you live in a larger home or have a few smaller spaces that have functioned as general catch-alls and storage. That's alright. Make a list of every area in your house by sitting down and using it as a tangible representation of your progress. Make a show of crossing a room off when you are through with it. Use a thick Sharpie to scribble over it or write over it. Find a quick and easy method to treat yourself, and then tell everyone how you organized and decluttered that area!

A major first step towards leading a minimalist lifestyle is decluttering your home, and you can also profit from the opportunity to donate many of your belongings to those who are less fortunate than you. Think about using this time to allow yourself to experience these memories and meditate on your emotional condition. Then, give yourself permission to realize that parting with these things does not equate to throwing away your memories. This implies that, just as you could, someone else can now profit from these things and make their own priceless memories.

The distinction between a genuine minimalist lifestyle and a commercialized minimalist lifestyle is the next item to comprehend.

Why does clutter accumulate?

The more we purchase, the more we accumulate wealth. We simply threw the old printer on the floor after we bought a new one because our old one ran out of toner. The robotic arm prototype is being compared to the filing cabinet. The designer hot patches from last season are draped over the pocket-sized print-it pad that we use for off-site notes. The leftover meatloaf container will be a delicious snack tonight as we watch the most recent episode of Natural Fluids, given an explanation.

The reason clutter accumulates is because it requires work to put things away. The first thing you need to do is turn to face the flirt. After that, you should consider what it is. After that, you truly need to pick it up and go the entire distance to where it goes in order to store it. It's possible that you'll need to take an entire journey for each item.

Multitask while storing the crater

While you're moving around, take out your headphones and music player, turn on an audiobook about optimizing supply chain management through value-added procedures that are essential to the ongoing paradigm shifts in your business, and become inspired. You'll organize both your space and your thoughts.

Clothing

Many of us find clearing the clutter intimidating, and it's interesting to investigate the cause of inertia. You might believe that women are the only ones who struggle with a curated wardrobe. The truth is that although women tend to be slightly more likely to experience a sexual assault, men and children can also experience this issue. The good news is that you will get numerous benefits when you declutter your wardrobe. You will be aware of the things you own, finding what you're looking for will be a lot easier, and it will add to the overall charm of your house.

Take everything that doesn't fit you anymore and put it in a box to sell on eBay or donate to a local charity. Now, let's see how many things there are and the ones that you no longer find appealing. Remove those items and place them inside the box. Keep your summer and winter clothes separate.

You may inevitably come across apparel pieces that you adore but never wear for specific reasons. Perhaps you don't want to wear short skirts any longer. However, if you purchase a lightweight, short-sleeved jacket or cardigan, you can choose to wear it again and again. Take out a piece of paper and pen, then list the items of clothing you need so that the clothes in your wardrobe will come back to life. Additionally, indicate the color that this garment should be.

Finding what you want when you want will be simpler when you organize your wardrobe. You won't lose money by replacing items you already own. Your clothing will be kept in more spacious and neater locations.

Day 5: How much will it set you back?

"The amount of life you exchange for anything is its price."

Thoreau, Henry David

"Everything that does not add value to your present life is costing you something" is the fundamental tenet of Japanese minimalism, as taught by Marie Kondo.

Try to figure out how much it will cost to create the life you desire on day five. Unintentionally, things that don't bring you joy or value are robbing you of happiness, value, and peace of mind.

Your daily task: On day five, remember that if something isn't making your life better or bringing you joy, it's detracting from it. As a result, you don't need it because it's not accomplishing anything constructive.

Day 6: "Remember your belongings"

"The magnitude of your belongings is not as significant as the depth of your experience #awakening #enlightenment #consciousness."

Sadhguru

Living a minimalist lifestyle involves being aware of your surroundings so that when you make decisions about what to own, you can quickly determine what makes you happy and adds value to your current life. Then, you can consciously decide to hold onto those things by getting rid of everything that detracts from or does not add value to your life.

Today's activities: Today's action is to adopt a new perspective on your belongings. To put it simply, simplifying your life involves planning each day carefully around a set of values that reflect your requirements and aspirations for the life you want to lead.

Chapter 1: A Lifestyle of Minimalism

If you're new to minimalism, you might believe that it means giving up all of our luxuries, but that's not the case. Minimalism is mostly about eschewing the exaggerated values and meanings we attach to items and pleasures, yet it also involves making the transition to a simpler, stress-free, and joyful life. Consider minimalism as a "zero waste life," in which we learn to be content with the essentials of life rather than accumulating an excessive amount of unnecessary items for both internal and external use. By practicing minimalism, we can learn to enjoy the freedom from overspending and stockpiling, from thinking about the things we own and desire, from the tension and anxiety that accompany these thoughts, and from feelings of guilt and melancholy associated with owning or not owning them. When we become minimalists, we essentially accept things as things; we don't give any object a specific significance; instead, an item's value and utility determine its worth rather than sentimental factors like who gave it to us, how much it cost, or how beautiful it is.

Being minimalist means trying to avoid the constant messages of "buy now, be happy" that come from the media and our culture, which exalts material possessions. Our culture has developed into one where excess and repetition are self-indulgent. In actuality, more material possessions cannot make us happier since true happiness originates from within and is something we must cultivate for ourselves. Realizing that the happiness we derive from possessing material goods is fleeting is crucial, and having this understanding can greatly assist in leading a minimalist lifestyle. Furthermore, minimalism might help us disconnect from life's problems and regrets from an unchangeable past, in addition to helping us appreciate certain situations. Put another way, minimalism enables us to cherish and recognize the most important times in our lives. Additionally, minimalism helps us become more conscious of the people and things around us by limiting our possessions to those that will make our lives easier. Basically, the concept is to have only those that are important. We could relieve the burden of possessing too much extra stuff, which can unintentionally affect our physical, mental, and emotional well-being, by reducing the amount of stuff we own.

"Simplicity is letting go of burdens and leading a lighter, less distracted life—as each person defines it—that does not compromise a high-quality life."- Linda Breen Pierce.

Although every one of us is unique and thus able to have our own perspective and personal definition of minimalism, the philosophy behind minimalism is the same: in order to have a high quality of life, we must free ourselves from the entangling distractions of life, as each of us defines it. By teaching us to be content with the necessities and a select few items, minimalism has the effect of lessening our burden. As we learn to be content with what we already have, we stop wanting more and start clearing similar thoughts from our minds, which helps us release the clutter of life and reduce stress. Furthermore, living a clutter-free existence enhances concentration, and fewer outside distractions provide the drive to do what's essential and significant. By concentrating on the most important components, we become more mentally and emotionally strong and gain a clear grasp of our own objectives and successes. To put it briefly, minimalism can be a means of making our lives more beautiful and simpler, and the path to simplicity can lead to living a significant and meaningful life.

We must examine our beliefs, ideologies, and inner selves in order to comprehend the minimalism principle and the reasoning behind it. For instance, we experience stress even after achieving our objectives as a result of working tirelessly to support ourselves financially. We'll shell out hundreds of dollars for clothing, décor, and other extravagances and thousands of dollars for other "wants" like toys and cars. We develop an obsession with accumulating material belongings, and this cycle of buying things keeps repeating itself. Eventually, we get mentally exhausted from the stress of never having enough and worrying about holding onto what we do have, which results in debt, clutter, and noise. Anxiety stemming from worries about our public image and perception eventually follows this process. As a result, we begin to link achieving happiness to accumulating wealth, amazing extravagance, and a luxurious way of life. These things provide us with momentary satisfaction, but they also cause us a great deal of worry. In an attempt to earn more money, we overwork and exhaust ourselves, becoming overly concerned about holding onto current luxury and prioritizing acquiring more. Therefore, even when we achieve our goals, we still long for more because, deep down, we know that superfluous luxuries will never truly satisfy our needs.

This problem has a perfect answer in minimalism, which can also help one achieve happiness, serenity, and inner peace. Let's investigate its suggestions.

The Reasons For Reading This Book

Without forcing you to throw everything away on the first day (because that is not the point!), this book will walk you through the process of discovering minimalism step by step.

If you're looking for a few-page minimalist guidebook that will help you achieve the required goals, you should also read this book. If a book about minimalism had hundreds of pages, would it still appear plausible?

They have attempted numerous attempts at cleaning up their mess and are living with it on a regular basis. You will ultimately succeed with minimalism.

We aspire to a simpler, more independent life with more time for the necessities.

Seek to locate the things and ideas that you genuinely love, need, and hold significance for you.

- envision yourself as organized and structured, with lots of time, a clear head, an uncluttered workstation and closet, a lightly furnished and well-kept wellness haven, and no worry.

Be cautious; after reading this book, you might find that you suddenly want to downsize from your existing flat because it's too big, or you might want to take less money out of your work pension because you won't need as much. You may want to start a new pastime or spend more time with pals. Or..?

Take Note: What Minimalism Is and Is Not

It seems like everyone is talking about minimalism these days. Although this way of life has long been established and practiced in the USA, its renown is gradually spreading throughout the world.

However, the word minimalism is often associated with negative connotations. Some people might believe that living with just a mattress rather than a whole bed, for example, is acceptable. Some contend that minimalism only permits the use of chilly, empty, and visually sterile surfaces. These incorrect perspectives come from minimalists listing on their blogs the hundred or so things they own.

It is evident that living a minimalist lifestyle can take this form, but it is merely one of many options. Minimalism: Arrangement Momentum Freedom takes a different route, comprehends minimalism as a tool, and shares it with others to enjoy greater freedom, time, and order. The tool functions as a filter, allowing only the significant and fulfilling aspects of life to pass through. The size of the passage through your filter is entirely up to you. But the opening must be large enough to allow for the passage of useless objects and ideas.

It's likened to a Zen garden. Everything is set up in a tender and exquisite manner. There aren't any parasitic weeds that consume the energy of other plants. Everything is in balance. However, it might just as easily be a large or tiny garden with a variety of species. Your minimalist garden is yours to tend to.

Are you beginning to understand the true meaning of minimalism? That's correct; the goal is to achieve greater order, time, and freedom by simplifying one's life to the point where one just concentrates on the lovely and important things, both inside and outside.

Critics of minimalism contend that while this way of living has many advantages, it also has many drawbacks, including dehumanization. Humans need chaos (as a stimulant to stimulate lateral thinking) for good functioning and productivity; total order, on the other hand, indicates a standstill. Hence, perseverance is essential for creativity, even when it's not convenient or enjoyable at the time.

Remain calm. Within minimalism, there is room for even spontaneous disorder—just not the kind that takes a lot of effort and time. It is not necessary to live in a meticulously tidy room like in a hotel (though it is certainly acceptable if that helps you feel better). Instead, minimalism encourages you to surround yourself with the most meaningful and beautiful things in life, both tangible and intangible, and to employ a variety of strategies to feel more time and fundamentally freer.

To reach this state, one must identify the disruptive weeds in the garden (obtrusive, pointless thoughts; items that hide the truly important; labor-intensive work methods, diversions, divagations, etc.) and remove them. After that, one must discover a technique that prevents the weeds from growing again and a fertilizer that promotes healthier plant growth. The minimalism that this book discusses will enable you to handle all of this. Allow inspiration to come to you, and then use that inspiration to shape your own life into a Zen garden where you can learn more about the three concepts of order, time, and freedom.

Learning About The Minimalist Theory

Bruno's comment, in my humble opinion, perfectly captures life with a dash of modern consumerism. We all know deep down that less is more, but society has made it difficult to accept this obvious principle.

Discarding the societal perception of minimalism

Before delving into the components of minimalist philosophy and its immense potential, let us set the record straight on the misconception you may currently hold about it. Many people simply observe the home's bare white walls and sparsely spaced modern items. Although this may represent an accurate picture of extreme minimalists, a typical minimalist's life does not resemble this.

I'm also here to tell those of you readers who believe the minimalist lifestyle is merely a fad or trend—it's much more than that. Although some individuals briefly experiment with living a minimalist lifestyle, it's important to remember that these individuals are also responsible for creating a false perception of what a true minimalist looks like. Thus, it's okay if you have to discard all of your prior knowledge of minimalism! We're going to impart the facts regarding this more straightforward lifestyle in this chapter.

First off, being minimalistic goes beyond simply starting to "give up 100 items that you own," starting to cycle 10 miles to work, or skipping employment in favor of traveling the world on foot. No, minimalism can actually help you achieve more in your personal life, which may eventually lead to being the stylish person who travels the world while working in your coziest beachwear.

A Simplifying Tool

The core idea behind minimalism is that it's a way of living that assists you in finding the means to reduce your possessions to the essentials, which is the actual first step towards contentment. You can achieve the kind of freedom in your life that enables you to let go of the things that burden you with needless worry and anxiety more easily when you practice minimalism. Less means more enjoyment of life!

As you go through your weekend chores, such as organizing, putting away, cleaning the bedroom, kitchen, garage, and so forth, you find yourself thinking back to a time when you spent that valuable weekend time not cleaning what you had but spending it with your children, engaging in new hobbies, starting a side business, and other activities. By getting rid of items you no longer need or never used in the first place, minimalism allows you to have more space and time for the activities you truly like doing. If you were to crush the materialistic culture, how would your life be? That vision can come true with minimalism!

Reconstruct the True Significance of Worth

Although owning material possessions is perfectly acceptable, there is such a thing as having too much stuff. We place far too much importance on the possessions we acquire because of the notions that commercialization and materialism have imposed on us in today's culture. Our upbringing has conditioned us to believe that possessing a large home, a fancy car, or other ostentatious possessions makes one deserving of respect or wealth. If your closet is filled with the newest styles, etc., you are regarded as the fashion queen.

In some way, the things we gather in life allow us to assume things about other people and ourselves. This is the box that humanity has been forced into by materialism. Isn't it time to start living the happier, more independent life we deserve and to stop succumbing to what society has taught us?

The truth is that your possessions—no matter how many or expensive they are—will never truly enrich your life. Consider this: you aren't going to flaunt your Land Rover in heaven after this life, are you?

This is not to mean, however, that you are not worthy of having pleasant things in your life. Naturally, we want to spend the money we earn on high-quality items since we have worked so hard for it! But before you go beyond the bounds of simplicity and value, there's a limit.

Possessing lovely stuff does not elevate you over your neighbors, family, or friends.

Getting Rid of the Social Fog

The idea behind minimalism is to pare down our possessions to what we truly need, leaving our brains and lives empty of everything else. This enables us to make important choices regarding our aspirations and ambitions, empowering us to pursue our actual aspirations rather than those that are swayed by materialism.

We can strive for bigger and better things in our lives rather than becoming fixated on material belongings when our brains are freed from the cloud that consumerism casts over us. Consider it as a tool to help you purge your life of all the extraneous and superfluous things, which will improve your capacity to concentrate on happiness, freedom, and fulfillment.

Step One

A minimalist lifestyle's central tenet is to get rid of items that are unnecessary to create space for those who are.

Individuals who are unfamiliar with this manner of living sometimes believe that minimalism entails selling everything. In actuality, there is more to it than people realize.

How, then, do you get started?

Deciding what matters and what doesn't in terms of people, stuff, and activities is the first step towards minimalism. Although it is really that easy, the real difficulty is that, like everyone else, you have actually lost sight of what is truly important. Certain insignificant items have gained significance, while others that ought to have been considered significant have been demoted to lower priority.

Minimalism is, in a sense, a return to the fundamentals—to choosing carefully and leading a purposeful life as opposed to letting things happen by themselves.

This is Just the Start.

Eliminating material belongings is not the only aspect of minimalism, but it's always an excellent place to start. Everything you own, no matter how big or tiny, is more than just ordinary possessions to you. These items are a part of your life; they all stand for different things: habits, ideals, aspirations, history, and desires.

That is difficult to let go for precisely this reason. For some, it may just be a tattered shirt, but for you, it holds memories spanning a lifetime and signifies a significant period in your life.

Usually, the beginning is the most difficult. Because there will be emotions involved, going through your belongings and deciding which ones you want to keep and which ones to give away can be quite painful.

Consider it therapy, as you will be addressing underlying feelings that you have been holding inside for a long time in addition to clearing out clutter from your environment.

Your home is an extension of your mind. In addition to getting rid of items that are unimportant, decluttering your mind also releases tension and thoughts that are superfluous.

It's Not Just a Maths Game

But remember that it's never just a maths game. Living a minimalist lifestyle does not mean having as few possessions as possible; rather, it means being aware of what you need and want in life. The goal of minimalism is to have just enough material possessions without sacrificing happiness or tranquility.

Tips For Getting Ready For Your Lifestyle Modification

Are you prepared to make the move? You might be starting something better today. Remember, there's no turning back once you start; giving up is never an option.

Make a commitment to change.

Getting committed is perhaps the easiest part of becoming a minimalist, as well as the most difficult. Without your wholehearted dedication, your life will never change. You cannot have others do it for you. It is up to you whether this endeavor succeeds or fails.

Decide to bring about that transformation!

Put your pledge in writing. "I will live with only the things I need going forward and get rid of the things I don't."

Allow these phrases to serve as a mantra that you may keep repeating until you truly believe them.

You are now prepared for step 2 once you have made the commitment to change.

Keep these things safe.

The next stage is to decide which items you want to keep and which to trash. The following list should only be used as a reference. Remember that each circumstance is unique.

You will only have access to the following for the next seven days:

Set aside enough clothing for a week. Even while you may believe you need more, you don't really. It might not seem conceivable right now, but you'll realize that you just need clothes for a week or so.

Take whichever little things are most meaningful to you. Certain items hold sentimental significance that is unquestionable. You may have a few pictures of your loved ones or this antique music box that was given to you when you turned eighteen. Because you feel like you can't get rid of everything, this can be difficult. The things themselves won't matter as much as the memories you hold dear. Letting go of the smaller things will make it easier to let go of the larger ones.

Save everything you require for your passion or pastime. It's possible that you enjoy music, in which case you should hold onto that special guitar. A bookworm will have a difficult time parting with their collection. People can now store all of their favorite books in one location with the help of technology; a laptop or tablet would be useful for this.

Preserve your laptop and smartphone. Depending on what you really need, this. Bring your laptop if it's a must for your job. The same is true for your smartphone. Perhaps you don't think much of them, but you do use them sometimes, so you should hold onto them.

Essentials of daily existence. Are all those knives and pieces of kitchen top necessary for your kitchen? Look inside your closet; there may be expired goods there. Take only the items you use every day. When choosing your toiletries, try to choose multipurpose things.

These may not seem like much, but if you take a closer look at your life, you'll undoubtedly find that you actually wear at least ten different outfits every six months. The remaining items, on the other hand, you may have worn only once or not at all. If you haven't used them in the previous six months, you might want to get rid of them.

Other Types OfDecluttering

A minimalist's lifestyle has a cascading effect. After you experience the advantages of having a tidy home and organized routine, you'll want to declutter even more. We will thus examine other areas of your life that require cleaning in this chapter.

Connections
Relationships that are toxic are among the worst types of clutter. You spend time worrying about someone, not having fun with life. You give this person the authority to dictate how happy you are.

In actuality, though, you can be happy without seeking approval from anyone.

But don't misunderstand the entire situation. The other person is not always bad just because a relationship is poisonous. There are situations when personalities just don't mesh well. Such partnerships are not necessary. Letting go of them is your greatest option.

Breaking up isn't simple, though. And if you've ever been through one, you might attest to this.

Try discussing your issues with the other party first. He or she might not even be aware of them.

Refrain from discussing this over the phone since it is really crucial. Additionally, prepare your remarks ahead of time before the meeting. The best method to make sure you don't overlook anything crucial is to do this.

But keep in mind that there are other people who have mouths. Allow your buddy or partner to share their perspective as well; you might also bear some of the blame.

After the talk, if nothing changes, it's advisable that you pack your luggage. This is typically a hard and challenging choice. However, as they say, one door shuts, and another opens.

Realizing that you are in charge of your happiness will come from ending a poisonous relationship. so that when you enter another one later on, you won't feel needy. Moreover, you'll know exactly what you want out of it.

Journeying

The amount of luggage individuals bring on their trips is shocking. You must make a change right away if you are guilty of this.

All this baggage does is cause you to move more slowly. You become distracted with moving, packing, and watching over things. If, after a vacation, you arrive home fatigued, that is.

Thus, begin learning to travel light today.

Three shirts, three pairs of pants, some pants, a shoe and some toiletries are enough to last a man. With the same amount of equipment, women will likewise function well.

You might also include a digital camera if it's a vacation. However, you don't necessarily need an entire bag of earrings or a laptop.

Money

The largest source of clutter in our lives is money. Therefore, investing time in effectively managing it makes sense. Here are some pointers on managing your finances like a minimalist.

Budget: Without one, you won't be aware of the expenses taking up your money. Additionally, there's a greater chance of straying from minimalism.

Wait until the end of the month before making any purchases; instead, put them on your budget. You can proceed with the purchase if you discover that you still need the item. However, you'll usually come to the conclusion that your purchases were impulsive.

Eliminate debt: A lot of people believe that debt may solve their financial woes. However, the contrary is actually true—it makes your issues worse.

You have to put in more effort when you owe someone. And yes, you guessed it—this adds more chaos to your calendar.

Spend less if you don't have any money. That is all there is to it.

It also helps to get rid of all of your credit cards.

Having an emergency fund should be your lifesaver in difficult circumstances. Regrettably, beginning to save is difficult, just like forming any healthy habit. You constantly come up with a reason not to do it.

However, let me offer you some advice: now is the best moment to begin saving money.

Put any raise you receive into your emergency fund. Additionally, you can request that your bank automatically deposit a portion of your income to your fund.

Don't have more than two bank accounts; it may feel wonderful to have many accounts open in your name. Regretfully, taking care of all of these takes time. Setting a two-account limit is one way to address this.

The Goods AndBads Of Minimalism

"Acquire more, exert more. Improve yourself. Many ads, motivational speeches, and self-help books boil down to these few words. Purchase more of those elegant outfits and up-to-date personal care items if you wish to look excellent. Increase your level of leisure activity if you want to feel excellent. Enhance your own quality of life before attempting to improve others. Increase your output. Exercise greater caution. Never stop trying to improve upon who you were the day before.

Every year, a plethora of goods, services, and initiatives are created to carry on those ostensibly benign maxims. As a result, you have a wide range of possibilities for goods to use, services to obtain, and things to try. Making a selection could be stressful, so you attempt to obtain and interact with as many of them as you can. Long shopping lists and bucket lists are telltale indicators that you've given in to temptation. Additionally, your messy home acts as a reminder.

Global waste management is a challenge that is made worse by the "more is better" mentality. Purchasing more items means you will have more to discard now or in the future. There will still be a lot of garbage produced even if only one million people in the world are materialists. Indeed, in 2017 alone, more than 100 million tonnes of solid garbage were disposed of in US landfills. Thousands of acres of land that may have supported wildlife are taken over by those dumps. Recall that those piles of trash used to be money as well.

Some people can easily discard a large amount of stuff, whereas others find it difficult to part with their clutter. Someone who suffers from a hoarding problem will retain anything, no matter how cheap and broken it is. The hoarder's movement within their own home is even impeded by the overwhelming amount of clutter. Damage to structures is also anticipated.

That just served to demonstrate that having more isn't always preferable. The tenet of minimalism is that less is more. The idea is essentially about learning to live with enough. Although it can be done, it isn't always done.

Reasons for the Preoccupation with Compiling

Large-scale implementation of minimalism might still be challenging, even in a different universe. Besides, who doesn't want lots of options? If the large selection includes the product of your dreams, you don't have to accept anything less. The process of experimenting with most or all of the alternatives can also be enjoyable.

One potential cause of hoarding is a love of options. You show this by maintaining wardrobe and shoe collections. Having both official and informal ones is only appropriate. Even so, you might still own separate outfits for traveling, working out, watching sports, going to concerts, and going on dates. Additionally, you might not want to appear as though you're always wearing the same pair of shoes and outfits. As a result, you own shoes, blouses, and outfits in various styles.

Possessing a variety of food and beverages at home is another indication that you value options. Coffee is available for breakfast as well as for moments when you need to stay focused. For movie marathons, there are chips and beverages available. Wine is available for happy occasions and difficult days. Additionally, you might be stockpiling chocolates or pastries to lift your spirits in case you're having a bad day.

When your options are limited, anxiety sets in. Additionally, the fear of losing out is what motivates you to acquire additional possessions.

As you already know, sales are mostly used to entice customers to make purchases rather than as a means of compensation. However, as year-end and Black Friday discounts become more commonplace, it appears that skipping them will cost you a lot of possible savings. But in really, all that's happening is that you're being duped into thinking you received more value for your money.

Marketers know you desire that sensation. In addition to bargains, they promote the illusion that you're saving a lot of money by giving away freebies and discounts. Many of them even go so far as to establish loyalty programs in which participants receive additional benefits. Such initiatives are well-known in retail businesses.

In order for loyalty programs to function, users must register. Payment may or may not be required for the application. It's not quite free, though; in order to become a member, you might have to make a certain number of transactions. Afterwards, a membership card is typically given.

The advantages take time to manifest. Points are meant to be earned by you first. You can accrue those points by making purchases from the company that issued the card. To get the greatest offers, you must have a lot of points. You must spend a lot of money on a lot of unnecessary items if you want to score highly. You will eventually become impatient with the procedure. You can stop using the card or end your membership completely. But you will not be able to recover the lost funds.

Another thing that makes you want to keep buying is convenience. Producers and merchants promote large purchases by creating the impression that it would be too difficult to restock every few months. Yes, there is truth to what they say. You don't want to spend hours caught in traffic merely to get to the market and back home if you live in a populated city. Shopping in crowded marketplaces and navigating their limited supply can be unpleasant as well.

So, you stock up on food, drinks, and hygiene to avoid those problems. If you dislike doing laundry at least once a week, you may have thought about purchasing additional clothing, stockpiling a lot of fragrance items, and experimenting with fast spot removers. Purchasing spares and replacements are also advised so that you are ready for any eventuality.

Having a backup laptop allows you to continue working in the event that your primary laptop breaks, delaying repair work until later. If you keep a portable fridge in your bedroom, you may easily reach for a snack or drink when you're hungry or thirsty at night. You could watch until you nod off. What would happen if your friends asked you to throw a party at your house? If you have multiple dishes, cups, and utensils that have been stored in your cupboards for a long time, you'll feel comfortable.

Though you might not be interested in crafts today, you might be in the future. Keeping craft supplies stored makes sense. These days, your automobile, furniture, appliances, clothes, and other items you use frequently can be in good shape. Nevertheless, harm to them is inevitable at some point. Even though you aren't familiar with using most of the repair kits, be ready for such an eventuality by having some in your car and at home.

It's supposedly not a wise decision to not plan for every possible outcome. On the other hand, being prepared for possible annoyances is sensible and practical. The fast stain removers are advertised as time-efficient products. But did it ever occur to you that purchasing, storing, and getting rid of them can also be hassles?

As a shopper, you should not just look for offers that seem amazing but also monitor trends. Almost every industry forecasts trends that will come back and forth. Many are tenable but not always helpful. Consider the suede sectional chair craze of 2010. It was promoted as a less costly option to furniture with leather upholstery. Suede's attraction, meanwhile, was short-lived. It is, after all, difficult to maintain. These days, it's a material that's mostly used for smaller pieces of furniture, such as dining chairs and three-seater couches.

The possibility of the suede sectional chairs returning exists. The infamous avocado green fad of the 1970s cannot be justified in the same way. To be honest, warm hues of fall were in vogue back then. The benefit of the mustard yellow and burnt orange kitchen appliances that were popular at the time was that they went well with brick and wood surfaces. As of right now, finding anything to go with gas ranges and avocado green refrigerators is still really difficult.

The fact that celebrities push pointless goods and fads doesn't help. Among those goods are Cristiano Ronaldo's facial exercise device and Gwyneth Paltrow's vaginal eggs. Positively, the majority will not purchase such due to the ridiculousness of such creations. Sadly, a lot of people are tricked into purchasing allegedly authentic goods from well-known actors, TV series, games, and films.

The fan base puts pressure on you to purchase both the performer's physical and digital records if you're a fan. Next, when you go to concerts, record videos and take pictures so you may share them later on social media. Organize props and dress up for the occasion to provide extra special touches. Additionally, extra goods are available just outside of the venues.

These are insignificant in comparison to the official and unofficial movie franchise memorabilia. The most popular ones are T-shirts and posters. Additionally, there are shoes, hats and bags bearing the names and logos of those movies. Many manufacturers attempt to reach a broader market by imprinting brand names on practical products like bed linens, tumblers, and umbrellas. Then there are the pointless things like stickers, action figures, and books that tell behind-the-scenes tales.

In addition to the entertainment sector, the fashion business is also at the forefront of identifying and repurposing trends that are typically unfeasible. While superstars may seem stylish in their tailored three-piece suits, office workers may not even fit into their mass-produced equivalents. Pop stars and children alike would probably look good in such vividly colored trousers. If you don't know how to match outfits or have a personal stylist, you'll look tacky and feel self-conscious when wearing trousers that make a statement.

As if those aren't enough, world-maximalist fashion is making a comeback thanks to well-known labels. In addition to trousers in vibrant colors, bold designs are also becoming more and more popular. Remember to add layers, frills, and embellishments.

It's plausible to argue that the 2010s saw a rise in the popularity of minimalist fashion, which helped make way for its maximalist opponent. (Nonconformists will likely advocate for the opposite when something is receiving so much attention. That is typical.) Statement piece enthusiasts often minimize the former, calling it uninteresting. They are able to draw attention to their tastes through maximalist dress. Wearing muted hues and eschewing embellishments, on the other hand, are regarded as unimpressive.

The greatest thing about the maximalist movement may be that its increasing acceptance indicates that there is an issue with minimalism becoming a fad. It is advantageous if fewer items are purchased and used by all. It's ironic that designers strive for minimalism when creating different kinds of items. The idea becomes tarnished mostly due to its commercialization.

Simple designs and solid colors are characteristics of minimalist clothing. It also includes seamless gowns, shirts, and undergarments. The only item that is permissible is a wristwatch. (If you're married, it's acceptable to maintain your wedding band.) Neutral colors are favored greatly for shoes and purses. In minimalist style, patches, sequins, and studs are out of style.

A fast search for minimalist houses on Pinterest will provide pictures with clear countertops, thin furniture, and white walls. Then, there are minimalist décor options designed to keep your house from appearing run-down. To liven things up, add framed pictures, creative planters, pendant lights, elaborate mirrors, and multicolored throw pillows.

These facts, however, do not imply that you are a minimalist just because you own objects labeled as such. Being an avid moviegoer and purchasing official goods does not necessarily make one the greatest fan. Donating fashionable clothing won't make you look respectable or fashionable—rather, it will only make you a conformist. Regardless of the quantity of items you maintain in your house, you will never be ready for every eventuality. Say to yourself, "Enough."

Release Time From Your Schedule

A busy schedule that is overflowing with deadlines and assignments is detrimental to both mental and work-life balance. There is just so much that we can handle at once. We will only become more worn out every day if we are always on the move and never take a break. We eventually experience burnout. Everything requires a lot more work than it ever has, and even simple chores become nearly hard to complete. Our capacity for productivity can be severely compromised by burnout, which can also push us towards procrastination. Procrastination exacerbates the already hectic schedule we already have. As we list everything we need to accomplish, our minds become cluttered, and we lack the motivation to complete any of it.

As we started organizing our calendars, the pile of work that was about to overwhelm us got smaller every day. We begin doing only the things that truly need to be done rather than having a mound of duties waiting for us every day. This gives us more free time and improves our ability to manage our time. Completing tasks is equally vital as decompressing. Our job will decrease in quality if we are under constant stress. We can feel refreshed and at ease when our schedules are freed up, and we take pauses. This motivates us to work harder rather than being "lazy." Small tasks no longer divert our attention, and we no longer experience chronic burnout. We now possess the drive and vigor necessary to take on the significant tasks we have been putting off. Our productivity increases, and we have more time to spend with friends and family.

We can also improve our attitudes about work by decluttering. When you're always busy, taking on new tasks seems like a chore. Since you have to figure out how to fit new tasks and duties in with everything that is currently on your to-do list, you detest receiving new assignments and responsibilities. Any new work becomes less of a burden and more of an opportunity when you eliminate some of the irrelevant ones and leave yourself less to do each day. Because we feel like we're choosing to pursue these activities rather than having them thrust upon us, we begin to get passionate about work and other pursuits again. More control over our lives and daily routines makes us want to complete even the most difficult jobs because we are enthusiastic about the results. Since we care deeply about the task's completion, we have consciously chosen to dedicate ourselves to it. This sense of empowerment over oneself makes tough tasks much more tolerable.

Get Rid of Looping Thoughts

We offer ourselves a lot to ponder when our minds are overly full. Our thoughts might become loud and disruptive if we dwell on the hectic day we just had, consider what lies ahead of us tomorrow, or are just drawn away by something in our immediate surroundings. These thoughts clog our heads, making it difficult to concentrate on anything. It's possible for us to find ourselves daydreaming and hardly focusing on what's in front of us. This guarantees that we are unable to give something our whole attention, even when we are attempting to unwind or work on something. Because of the thoughts that won't go away, we wind up undermining ourselves by doing things halfheartedly. When we're working, occasionally, our flow of thinking veers off course, which can lower the caliber of our output. When we try to unwind, thoughts of the obligations we're putting off keep interrupting our leisure time and making stress flare up again.

When your circling thoughts follow you into bed, they can be very bothersome. If you're someone who overthinks things a lot, you've definitely worried yourself sick in the past. Every time you attempt to close your eyes and relax, anxiousness keeps interrupting your thoughts. You think about something that went wrong earlier in the day or something you have to do tomorrow that is already stressing you out. Your cranium is constantly jostling with ideas, causing you to be startled back to wakefulness whenever you are close to dozing off. If things in your life don't slow down, this might even start happening every night. Chronic insomnia, which reduces the amount of sleep you receive each night and leaves you feeling nearly exhausted, can be brought on by overthinking. It is especially undesirable to drift through the next day in a barely perceptible fog, particularly if your schedule is as disorganized as your thoughts.

You can focus throughout the day and sleep better at night by clearing your mind of these racing ideas. It is much simpler to calm your thoughts when they aren't racing from one thing to another and remind you of all the things that are causing you anxiety. Your mind won't become cluttered again, and you'll feel rejuvenated and prepared to face any challenge life presents the following day.

Minimise Everything in Your Diet

People frequently associate minimalism with the objects in our surroundings, but it also has to do with nutrition and eating habits. Here's how to incorporate minimalism into your diet:

Reduce the number of proteins: Use smaller plates at home, cut your meal in half while dining out, and refrain from getting second helpings when eating protein.

Reduce the amount of unhealthy meals you eat: Reduce the extra toppings and concentrate on increasing the amount of fruits and vegetables in your diet.

Reduce your snacking: Make an effort to avoid snacking, and when you do, choose nutritious foods like apples or carrots or eat smaller snacks.

Reduce the number of drinks you consume. Water is the best option for minimalists. Cut back on soda, cola, pop, soft drinks, and cake in favor of mostly drinking water. Stay away from diet beverages and only drink water.

Since they don't contain any nutrients, avoid them. Although they taste wonderful, people consume them despite the fact that they are bad for their weight and general health.

Cutting back on your diet has several advantages. A can of soda, for instance, has 240 calories. Two cans of beer equals over 500 calories, without including the calories from your major meals. Riding a bike for one hour and twenty minutes will burn approximately these calories. Therefore, you are effectively minimizing your life and workload by cutting back on your diet and emphasizing simplicity. Furthermore, since low-calorie diet beverages employ artificial coloring and flavorings, you are not allowed to consume them.

Organizing Your Thoughts

A minimalist lifestyle really benefits from mental decluttering. Mind cleaning and decluttering are achievable with patience and practice. Here's how to do it:

Swap out the negative ideas with constructive ones: Positive thought replacement is one of the best methods to clear your mind. Because of the way your brain is wired, thinking negative things like "I am sloppy and lazy at work" or "I am ineffective and ugly, and my partner/friend/coworker don't like me" might be problematic. Saying "stop" every time the critic enters your head is a highly powerful technique to break the cycle of negative thinking. Say "stop" or

"I'm not going there" if your mind wanders to a negative place. Concentrate on thinking positively, such as about your upcoming football game with friends or the nutritious dinner you'll be having tonight.

Embrace thankfulness: Sometimes the bad things you think are true. Making a gratitude list of the things and experiences in your life is one of the simplest methods to take your mind off of the disappointments in it. Thank God that you have fresh opportunities every day. Appreciate that you have a reliable job.

Act with awareness: Refrain from wasting your energy on excessive contemplation and fretting. Put your focus into thinking positively and acting in a helpful manner. Don't conceal yourself under sorrow, remorse, or irritation. Focus on the following constructive action instead. Put your money, time, and effort into finding a workable answer.

Decide when to worry: Decide when to worry. For instance, thirty minutes each night. Save all of your worrying till that moment, and then worry about the things that are bothering you.

Meditation: It helps to simplify life to live in the present moment without worrying about the past or the future. You may simplify and declutter your thoughts by practicing meditation.

The Republic of the Dominican

I did not visit Mexico. Though I had been there, I was unable to go this time. Although I had Mexico in my sights, fate had other ideas. My friend had attempted to convince me several times to relocate to Santo Domingo, Dominican Republic, where he had been living for a few years. He had attempted to persuade me to relocate to California when I was living there, but I had another buddy in Miami, Florida, who had made similar attempts. My acquaintance from Florida told me he could definitely get me a full-time position working for him on Everglades conservation. I was offered $600 a week by him. I thanked him and turned down his offer with grace. "No, but thank you so much!" was my response to my two buddies. My desire was to be in California.

When I was ready to travel again after recovering from my year in California, my Florida friend had moved on to something else in a different state. My acquaintance remained in Santo Domingo and had no intention of leaving anytime soon. We used to communicate virtually every day online, and one day, he was able to persuade me to relocate to the Dominican Republic and live close to him. He convinced me to make the move after we spoke about it for hours. We discussed almost all of my worries and objections, and he dispelled them all. I had decided to move to Santo Domingo by the end of the day.

After I made up my mind, the rest of the experience was like when I was getting ready to move to Arizona or California. I wrote a list of everything I would have to do, a small list of things I would need to buy, and a big laundry list of things I would need to get rid of. My intention was to take a one-way flight down there and spend at least half a year or more there. I had little money and had no idea where I would live. I would have to travel light, I knew. I had to pare down all I owned until I could fit into two bags.

One checked bag and one compact carry-on duffel bag.

A passport was simple to obtain. My auto insurance was simple to cancel. It was also simple to "lend" my mother my car, which they could either keep for me or sell if they needed the money. It was difficult to say goodbye to my friends and family, but they understood that I was doing what was right for me and would bring me happiness.

Trying to squeeze everything I owned into two bags was one of the hardest things I've ever done. For me, it was a kind of turning point. It seemed to me like one step towards homelessness. Particularly because I had just $1,800 (USD) in my bank account and was relocating to a different nation, I was a little alarmed by the modest amount, but I soon realized that $1,800 was a significant amount of money. Sufficient to last me many months till I could secure a source of income. After opening a new checking account at a different bank that provided free international ATM transactions, I transferred almost all of my funds from my previous account to the new one. I had $120 (USD) in cash stashed in my duffle bag in addition to the small amount of money I still had in my previous account. Even though the $120 in cash was ultimately taken, I still managed to move to a nation I had never been to with roughly $2,000. Some thought I was crazy, but I saw it as a wonderful chance to live overseas, visit my friends, and get better at Spanish.

Moving to a developing nation with $2,000, packing up everything you own into two bags, having no employment leads, and having only one good lead on a place to live is about as minimalist as it gets. I should say, one dubious lead on a rental property. I was to rent a room from the building's landlord in the spacious third-floor apartment with three bedrooms. The landlord occasionally resided there, but his permanent abode was a house in the United States. He leased the flat to another guy, this one residing mostly in the United States. I spent roughly fifteen minutes on the phone with the landlord, who informed me that the rent for the next two months would be $425. I agreed, but I told him I would need to check the location out first. I didn't think to inquire about staying for more than two months because it sounded like such a great offer. He said yes after I accepted the arrangement, provided that I first had to meet with him and check the location. After pausing, he asked if I could send the money to him right now. I declined his offer. He stated it was okay when I repeated that I would need to inspect the property first. He informed me that his brother lived on the second floor and would let me into the flat when I arrived and that his wife would eventually come get the rent. His request for me to wire money made me uneasy, but I reasoned that I wouldn't have anything to worry about as long as I could rent the place for that amount and make the payment when I got there.

I had clothes in my black suitcase. T-shirts, button-up shirts, shorts, and jeans. To write and mail letters, I had pens, paper, and envelopes. I carried five or six thin, short books, including a copy of Of Mice and Men. The only reason I bring it up is that the protagonists of the tale similarly have simple lives. Socks, pants and more things were in my little black gym bag. It was very hot, so I never wore pants or even half the stuff I brought down there. Along with my passport, checks, and checkbook, I also brought toiletries. $120 cash was stashed away at the bottom of my checkbook box. Six $20 dollars, tucked away and folded into quarters.

I paid $99 for a one-way ticket and left for the Dominican Republic with a black suitcase, gym bag, black dress shoes on my feet, black boots knotted together by the laces and literally hanging around my neck (I figured I could buy sandals once I was down there), and the clothes on my black. Although my friend who had been living there promised me he would show me around, take me to various locations, and introduce me to some people, I was still a little concerned. I would be okay as long as I had somewhere to stay for a while.

Give Your Life Purpose And Unique Meaning

When you have exciting goals to look forward to and are full of ideas that improve your life in the present, life is truly remarkable. Here's how cultivating a minimalist attitude might help you achieve that.

Day 8: Let Go of Thoughts That Are Negative and Unhelpful

Every day, the average human mind processes 50,000 thoughts. Just 10% of these concepts and views are pertinent to our values and concerns. Having said that, we frequently fail to identify, comprehend, or pay attention to those thoughts. We also find ourselves clinging to a lot of negative emotions. In addition, we have a terrible habit of dwelling on the past or the future. This fills our minds with so many garbage ideas that it prevents us from focusing on the important matters at hand.

By day eight, you've gained a lot of knowledge about organizing your life and thinking about the important things. Focus on teaching yourself how to identify and get rid of negative thoughts and the labeling habit on this particular day. Replace any negative thoughts you catch yourself thinking with constructive ones. For instance, instead of thinking about how you won't do a task correctly, replace that negative idea with one that affirms your ability and accomplishment in the things you persist in pursuing despite obstacles.

If you notice that you are thinking about a particular cruel buddy all the time, try to replace those thoughts with ideas of their positive traits. You might also consider how the friend in question has previously assisted you in overcoming challenges. But if you have decided to cut that toxic influence out of your life because someone hasn't been kind to you, take action. If you find yourself thinking about him/her, try focusing on the people who are important to you instead.

You will begin to feel better as you let go of your critical ideas and opinions.

Additionally, practice concentrating more on the here and now. Make peace with all of the unpleasant recollections and regrets from the past that keep you from sleeping. Consider the ways in which putting your time and effort into the here and now will improve your quality of life. In this way, you will have a better life now and pave the road for a prosperous future. When you look at it this way, you find it easier to let go of unneeded worries and regrets, and you begin to live more in the moment.

Day 9: Set a Purposeful Objective

A worthwhile, inspiring objective gives your life purpose and influences it in a certain way. The Vijayan family resides in Kochi, India. They don't have a lot of money, but they have fulfilling lives. When they got married 45 years ago, they made the decision to make world travel their lifelong ambition. They opened a modest coffee shop and now serve 300–350 people a day with coffee. Their earnings are modest because their shop is not very well-known outside of their community, but they are on a goal to save $4 to $5 every day, and this has allowed them to travel to a few places across the world, such as Brazil and Sri Lanka.

Theirs is the ideal illustration of a minimalist lifestyle focused on a worthwhile objective that enhances their quality of life. Find something that works for you as well, then put your attention towards making it a reality. A compelling aim makes everything in your life feel immediately more planned and ordered.

Day 10: Express gratitude

Think back on the previous ten days and consider all the incredible transformations you have brought about in your life on the tenth day. Your life will be very different from what it was before you began this 10-day adventure, which will astound and fill you with gratitude.

Give thanks to the universe right now for all of your blessings, particularly the capacity to recognize the value of minimalism and make it a way of life. To feel fortunate and satisfied, make it a habit to express your thankfulness every day for three to five things in your life that make it worthwhile.

Even if the ten days are up, you still have the rest of your life to live. Continue using the procedures described here to properly structure your life.

www.ingramcontent.com/pod-product-compliance
Lightning Source LLC
Chambersburg PA
CBHW052157110526
44591CB00012B/1988